TATLINGS

TATLINGS

Epigrams
by Sydney Tremayne
The Drawings
by Fish

DAVID & CHARLES
Newton Abbot   London   North Pomfret (Vt)

British Library Cataloguing in Publication Data

Tremayne, Sydney
    Tatlings.
    1. Epigrams, English
    I. Title
    828'.9'1208   PN6281

    ISBN 0-7153-7908-9

Printed in Great Britain
by Redwood Burn Limited Trowbridge and Esher
for David & Charles (Publishers) Limited
Brunel House Newton Abbot Devon

Published in the United States of America
by David & Charles Inc
North Pomfret   Vermont 05053 USA

ILLUSTRATIONS

Frontispiece

Most women if they had to choose would ask for a clear complexion in preference to a clear conscience — 18

Men do not try to escape temptations; their only fear is that some temptation should escape them — 22-3

You can never forget a sin you have confessed — 28

Most women live for the present, and the handsomer the present the better they live — 33

Men always say that they loathe being flattered, but don't take any notice—no man has ever known that he was flattered — 38

Letters that should never have been written and ought immediately to be destroyed are the only ones worth keeping — 43

The husband who counts is the one who has something to count — 48

When you see an old man alone you are looking at something very sad. When you see an old man with a young woman you are looking at something rich — 53

What a woman wears reveals more than what she says — 58

INTRODUCTION

HEREIN THE FORTUNATE READERS WILL FIND THE HAPPY CONJUNCTion of two very brilliant young people, whose literary and artistic talents fit like the proverbial glove, or the musical and lyrical alliance of those immortals, Gilbert and Sullivan.

Never were epigrams more worthily illustrated, or more worthy of illustration. The *joie de vivre*, the humour and the human observation which run through this little volume, will I am sure make a great appeal to the public possessing or admiring those qualities.

I am proud to think that I was responsible for the journalistic débuts of both authors, whose work enriched the pages of *The Tatler* for some years, and that I have been honoured in being asked to write an introduction to their first collective effort.

E. HUSKINSON

Editor of *The Tatler*

SYDNEY TREMAYNE was the pseudonym of Sybil Taylor, who was born in 1890, the first child of John Taylor, Squire of Carshalton, then a little country village. With the advent of an heir the village was given a holiday and bonfires were lit. When a girl was born, the village was sent back to work and the bonfires were extinguished.

WITH WHAT may have been a delayed reaction, at nineteen she ran away—'to live in an attic and write'. And write she did—three novels: *Eve*, *The Broken Sign-post* and *The Auction Mart*. The first two were best-sellers, the third not so successful.

IN 1913 she married Roger Cookson, a racing driver with the Bentley team, but after World War I she ran away again, this time from her husband, taking her two daughters with her. This was when she turned to journalism and joined 'The Tatler'. From there she left to edit 'Eve' (before it became 'Britannia & Eve'), and was the film critic, fashion editor and beauty specialist; she was also writing a monthly article for 'The Tatler' called 'Nights Out'.

SHE RETIRED in 1938 and never wrote, or wanted to, again. During World War II she returned to Roger Cookson (to his immense surprise) and stayed with him until her death in 1963.

TATLINGS

THE LOOKING-GLASS reveals us as we are to ourselves; the Wine-glass reveals us as we are to others.

IF A MAN puts a woman on a pedestal someone else will help her down.

NO MAN gets what he wants, though some may get what they have wanted.

THE REASON that a love affair so seldom ends happily is that one of the lovers is generally unwilling for it to end at all.

NO ONE agrees with other people's opinions, they merely agree with their own opinions expressed by somebody else.

IT IS a poor doctor who cannot prescribe an expensive cure for a rich patient.

TO A WOMAN women are a sex and men an individual.

A WOMAN alone is not necessarily a temptation, if she were a temptation she would probably not be alone.

IF YOU GIVE a woman an opportunity, she will take everything else that she wants.

YOU ARE much nearer success when you are deplored than when you are ignored.

SO MANY young women have glibly promised their lovers that they would 'never change' and have been unrecognisable ten years later.

ONE MAN'S love is often only the bait with which another man is caught.

SOME PEOPLE contrive to make their 'silent suffering' simply deafening.

A WOMAN may have a small mouth and yet be able to open it very wide.

SOME people succeed in preserving a youthful appearance, but they show their age in their opinions.

ONE CAN forgive a person lying about one and possibly disprove them, but it is unforgiveable if they tell the truth; that is taking a mean advantage.

THE ONLY blows Fate seems to deal some people are slaps on the back.

A GIRL WHO spends her youth learning philosophy will almost certainly need it when her youth is spent.

AS SOON as a woman has put a man in her power she puts him out of her heart.

IF A PRETTY back view won't let you catch it up it has probably got a horrible face.

NOTHING unites people like a common sorrow, except, perhaps, a vulgar joke.

IT IS PROBABLE that if a woman cannot see the point of her husband's jokes she will see very little indeed of him.

A WOMAN IS not really adequately clothed because she is draped in mystery.

WOMEN have been the same through all the ages: the only difference between a girl and her mother is their feeling for her father.

SOME PEOPLE drain the cup of life, and others stick to a medicine glass.

A WOMAN likes to know what the man she loves was like when he was a little boy; but a man would rather know what the woman he loves will be like when she is an old woman.

A MAN'S 'for ever' is just about as long as a woman's 'five minutes.'

SOME MEN borrow a fiver and behave for ever after as if the only thing they owed you was a grudge.

AMBITIONS vary: Men may want to do well, women may want to look well, but the old only want to sleep well.

WHAT a woman costs and what she is worth are two entirely different things.

A WOMAN cares most for a man when their love affair is over, a man cares most for a woman before their love affair has begun.

IT IS difficult for a man to understand that a woman who would go through hell for love of him is capable of leaving him because he clears his throat or uses a toothpick.

THE MEANS to an end may put an end to one's means.

A WOMAN'S clothes should be like an epigram, an adequate expression of an idea without a superfluous — syllable.

HE WHO CAN does, he who can't is shocked.

MANY A MAN has ended by running away with a woman because he had not the sense to begin by running away from her.

IT TAKES a clever man to write a good love letter, but only a fool would do it.

EVERYONE likes to be run after, but the difference between men and women is that men do not want to be caught and women do.

A WOMAN who can bear to hear her husband praise another woman is either different to other wives or indifferent to her husband.

IT IS inexplicable, but undeniable, that a man often prefers the woman he has to make excuses for to the woman he has to make excuses to.

TO BE successful in love one must know how to begin and when to stop.

ODDLY enough the impression made by the possession of several different names is not nearly so favourable as the impression made by the possession of several different addresses.

A ROMANCE is wonderful while it lasts, but if it lasts it ceases to be a romance.

WOMEN who are the easiest to win are always the most difficult to lose.

IT IS THE MAN who has no right who generally comforts the woman who has wrongs.

THERE ARE three stages in a man's infatuation for a woman: making his way, having his way, and going his way.

AN INFALLIBLE way of acquiring a host of friends is to be a host yourself.

MANY AN impecunious stylist has found that a girl is more easily won by an ordinary bank-note than an extraordinary love note.

MANY A WOMAN'S undoing is due to her maid.

WHEN A MAN is lost to one woman it is generally because he has been found by another.

A MAN MAY BE legally attached to one woman and yet sincerely attached to another.

IT IS perfectly saintly to love some women; and that presumably is sacred love. It is perfectly natural to adore others; and that probably is profane love.

BY ALL MEANS tell a woman you love her, but don't tell her anything else.

TO INDULGE in independent ways one really needs to have independent means.

IT IS no use collecting notable acquaintances unless you can be sure that they will recollect you.

MOST WOMEN if they had to choose would ask for a clear complexion in preference to a clear conscience.

THAT A MAN and woman are always together proves nothing—but it is probably true.

IF YOU CANNOT be funny without being shocking, it is better to be shocking.

OF COURSE it is quite dreadful to lead another into mischief, but it is almost impossible to enjoy oneself alone.

IF A WOMAN goes too far with a man, she comes back alone.

A PRETTY woman in a becoming gown is a temptation—men love temptations.

NOTHING is more infuriating than to be accused of doing something which one has taken every precaution to keep secret.

THE WOMEN who have nothing to show are the ones who have nothing to hide.

IF ONE lives long enough one is bound to become respectable and virtuous—hallowed by time.

WOMEN are always asking questions and men are always inventing answers —and women are none the wiser.

LOVE IS NICE when it is new, but it wears badly and is impossible to renovate.

GOODNESS is only a relative term, and one that is always on the tongue of relatives.

THERE ARE two sorts of lovers— those who forget and those who are forgotten.

EVEN THE MOST upright man may be tempted by a recumbent woman.

ONE SOON gets tired of saying a thing over and over again if nobody contradicts, just as one soon gets tired of doing a thing over again if no one says one mayn't.

EVERYONE must take chances and if they turn out right they are renamed opportunities.

A WOMAN'S accounts of how she spent 'the house money' are only equalled in inventive genius by a man's accounts of how he spent his time.

A WOMAN may have no reticence about her ankle or even her knee if it is pretty, but she will never show her hand.

MANY a woman has waited patiently for years until the man could afford to marry her, and then he won't wait patiently for five minutes while she puts her hat on.

SOME MEN consider marriage an unnecessary expense, and some men simply won't consider it at all.

A MAN will forgive a woman doing everything at his expense except making a joke.

FLIRTATION and office work are the oil and water which the devil sometimes tempts a man to attempt to mix.

IT IS ONLY a very great man who, in a higher position, does not look small to the man down below.

BY ALL MEANS express an opinion but not by post.

IT'S A MISTAKE to take a man into your confidence. If you do you will probably never trust him again and he will certainly never trust you again.

MEN do not try to escape temptations; their only fear is that some temptation should escape them.

IT'S A splendid plan to make a man run after you, but remember that he won't go on running indefinitely merely out of curiosity or hope. The time will come when he will sit down to rest—with someone else.

A WOMAN'S MIRROR reflects her whole world.

IT IS no good laying down the law if you can't take up an argument.

IF A WOMAN HAS anything worth telling she tells it; if a woman has anything worth showing she shows it.

IF A WOMAN'S appearance is bad her re-appearance is worse.

ALL BEAUTIFUL things are created for and destroyed by women.

A WOMAN who knows just when and how to make a scene is clever, but the woman who knows just when and how not to make a scene is wise.

PEOPLE who allow their character to be diluted by other people's opinions are naturally weak.

A WOMAN always puts on silk stock-ings before she takes the final step.

NO MATTER how orderly she is by nature it is a mistake for a woman to be always putting her husband in his place.

THERE never was a woman so fast that man could not keep pace with her.

YOU CAN'T be even acquainted with love without becoming intimate.

IF A HUSBAND leaves his wife alone ten to one someone else won't.

YOU will probably be very nearly right if you judge men by their hand shakes and women by their kisses.

ALCOHOL is not a good preservative of grey matter.

THE potentialities of a strong silent man are nothing to the potentialities of a weak talkative woman.

'PLATONIC friendship' is the story a woman puts up to a man before, and to the world afterwards.

SOCIETY says, if you have come into money you can come in anywhere.

IT IS a funny thing that a man always has to tell a woman that he loves her while everyone else knows it without being told.

SO MANY more people are capable of being loved than are capable of loving.

IF A MAN is free to do what he likes he does it; and if he is not free—he does it just the same.

BECAUSE she is up-to-date you must not count on a woman being up to time.

LOVE affairs are all alike, it is only the lovers who are different.

MARRIAGE is a woman's entry into and a man's exit from life—that is, officially.

HAVING what you want is not nearly so interesting as getting what you want.

THERE are two sorts of men, those who are constant in love and those who are constantly in love—and perhaps the first don't exist.

IF YOU don't want tummy-ache don't eat unripe fruit; and if you don't want heartache don't marry a young man.

THERE is only one temptation in the world that it is worth while resisting and that is—spring onions.

MONEY talks, and the larger the means the clearer the meaning.

ONE may get what one deserves but seldom what one is promised.

THE only time a thing is really worth doing is for the first time and for the last time.

THE WOMAN who has never deceived her husband must have an extraordinarily acute husband.

YOU can never forget a sin you have confessed.

THE education system must be all wrong. What sort of use is Latin to a young man on his first trip to Paris? You can't get much for'arder with a living woman by being familiar with a dead tongue.

EVERY woman should be an *édition de luxe* of herself.

IT IS MORE or less true that an attractive woman has no friends. The men are more and the women less.

IF MEN could read women's thoughts publishers would die of starvation.

WHAT a lovely world it would be if one could recover the money and the love and the time one has misspent.

IF A WOMAN is young and pretty and fascinating, the world of men will forgive her anything—and see to it that there is everything to forgive.

MEN will pretend to understand things that they don't and women will pretend not to understand things that they do.

THE one woman in the world who could make a man of a fool, a home of a house, and a romance of a marriage probably wears glasses and jaeger and so never gets a chance.

A MAN keeps a woman's love by making promises he can't keep; a woman keeps a man's love by refusing to make promises she can keep.

MANY women who look ripe are rotten at core.

IT IS no good having strong desires if you have a weak will.

THEY say that one way to continue to enjoy dinners for two after marriage is to have breakfast for one.

MANY a man makes a profession of being entertaining in order to be entertained.

MANY a woman who looks light would be a terrible burden.

A MAN does not ask a woman if she loves him until he is almost sure that she does so, and a woman does not ask a man if he loves her until she is almost sure that he does so no longer.

IF ONLY the women we love were as true as the things they teach us about women!

THE things one does because one wants to do them are generally wrong from somebody's point of view. It is therefore better to do them out of view of everybody.

A WOMAN likes the things her lover likes, but loathes the things he loves.

ONE is forgotten even sooner when one is alive than when one is dead.

A PRETTY woman alone is invariably considered a mystery; a plain woman alone is a perfectly natural phenomenon.

THE man who cannot make a mistake never tried.

WOMEN are generally supplied with the necessary food of life but they help themselves to salt.

ODDLY enough the woman who looks most self-possessed generally belongs to some man.

IF YOU don't tell a woman she will find out; and if you do tell a woman you're a fool.

EVERYONE has his own particular way of making an ass of himself and if your method is peculiar enough you are snapshotted for the halfpenny press—and that is fame.

FLIRTATION is the froth on top of the wine of love.

IT IS the most difficult thing in the world to attract the attention of a crowd, it is always so absolutely intent on the man who is trying to escape its attention.

A WOMAN may weigh thirteen stone and still love lightly.

A MAN sometimes wants to be alone to be alone, but if a woman wants to be alone it is to be alone *with* someone.

EVERYTHING depends upon position—even in the matter of adipose tissue.

THE people who are quite unforgiving are those to whom there is never anything to forgive.

IT DOES not matter that a kiss is ill-timed if it is well placed.

MOST women live for the present, and the handsomer the present the better they live.

ONE imagines that the reason some people are so keen on getting married is that you can't get divorced till you are married.

IF YOU want people to take your hand put it in your pocket.

EVERYONE goes everywhere now-a-days; it is very tiresome, because it makes it almost impossible to see life without being seen.

IF YOU can't get rid of a man any other way—marry him.

MEN all lie to women—in order to win them, in order to lose them, or sometimes only in order to comfort them.

SOME women's love stories are not even founded on fact.

I WONDER who suggested an apron string as the one to which a woman ties a man? In reality she would probably use a pink ribbon.

MOST women's ideas are better than their morals.

WOMEN are reputed to be able to do or undo anything with a hair pin. Some of them can do quite a lot without one.

LIFE is a guessing competition and the men who guess right become millionaires or misogynists.

WHAT a woman's eyes tell a man, and what his own eyes tell him is all he can ever hope to know about her.

NOTHING in this world is compromising until it is found out.

A GREAT scandal is generally the public version of a great secret.

RICH FRIENDS are a great expense; one is so apt to live beyond their means.

THERE is all the difference in the world between being left by oneself and being left by someone else.

ALL WOMEN want real love, but their passion for bargains leads them to accept cheap imitations.

MANY A MAN known to the public as a 'man of letters' is known to his own people as a man of casual notes and infrequent telegrams.

ALMOST anyone can be noticeable, but only a very few are distinguished.

YOU can't have a really good time and a really good reputation, but then a good reputation is of no value at all until it is lost.

IT IS extraordinary how marriage changes a man—towards the woman he has married.

A MAN will forgive a woman for not being there when he wanted her, but never for being there when he did not want her.

THE only way to close some people's mouths is to fill them.

THE man to marry is not the man you can be happy with but the man you can't be happy without.

HUSBANDS and wives often become fast simply in their efforts to escape one another.

IF A WOMAN expresses admiration for another woman, either she does not admire her or her husband does not.

THE FRENCH describe a woman of over forty as of a ' certain age,' but as a matter of fact it is after she is forty that a woman's age becomes most uncertain.

MOST PEOPLE are only caricatures of their own possibilities.

EVERYONE likes to be loved, if it is only to convince someone else that they are lovable.

WHEN a woman is past the love stage she is dead.

INFIDELITY is, very occasionally, the greatest compliment a man can pay a woman.

THE WOMAN who bares her shoulders usually has a larger following than the woman who bares her soul.

IT IS IMPOSSIBLE to study life and your husband as well.

MEN always say that they loathe being flattered, but don't take any notice—no man has ever known that he was flattered.

THE WORLD is logical and ruthless in its conclusions; it says that if a man is not worth any money he is worthless, and that if a man is worth £100,000 he is worthy.

THE BENEFIT of credit is greater than the benefit of the doubt.

A MAN who begins by asking a woman to sell her soul usually ends by asking her to sell her diamonds.

DISCRETION is the talent some women have of knowing with whom they can be indiscreet.

THE MOST perfect form of flattery is to tell people what they think of themselves.

WOMEN may want to be slaves but they insist on choosing their own masters.

THE CLEVEREST woman is not the one that can make a man feel that he is a fool but the woman that can make a man feel that he is a man.

A GOOD REASON MAY be a bad excuse.

MEN ARE capable of the most marvellous self-sacrifice; a man will even give up the woman he loves because he cannot afford to keep both a wife and a motor.

IT IS NOT her sense but his senses that make a man love a woman.

BE SURE that you are outside when you lock the door of the house of memory and throw away the key.

THE LAWYER'S Progress—getting on, getting honour, getting honest.

IF YOU want to keep a man's love, by all means dress for him, not before him.

LEADERS of men have been known to be followers of women.

THE LESS women care about clothes the more clothes they wear.

IT IS NOT what you think of him, but what other people think of your husband decides whether you have made a good match or not.

IN A CRISIS a woman will turn to a priest or a palmist.

DECEPTIONS are the oil to the wheels of life.

A MUTUAL sense of superiority is a good basis for friendship between two women.

LIFE for a man is getting and forgetting, for a woman giving and forgiving.

WHEN a man ceases to be single he *ipso facto* begins to lead a double life.

IT IS WELL to be out of reach but you must also be within sight to hold a man's attention.

WOMEN love men for their faults—when they can't find anything else to love them for.

A MYSTERY does not become a scandal until it is solved.

SOME people seem to think that a reputation for wit is to be gained by saying what they think; they forget that it is necessary first of all to think wittingly.

SILK stockings are the last things a woman discards—when she is economising.

GOOD habits are generally affectations or obesity cures and bad habits are often one's sole plea to personality.

MANY a man gets on his feet by continuing to lie.

ONE of the most adorable rules of life is always to put off till to-morrow what you are obliged to do to-day.

A LOVE affair that never ends is one that has been interrupted.

THE one that does not come out of a love affair well is the one that gets left in.

A WOMAN may have her price yet some one is always ready to give her away.

L ETTERS that should never have been written and ought immediately to be destroyed are the only ones worth keeping.

LOVE is a thirst that one cannot quench without becoming intoxicated.

IF YOU start making a man give up things you are almost sure to end by being one of the things he gives up.

IF YOU can't talk about a person behind their back, when can you talk about them?

IT IS NOT as a rule until a woman should really be in the past tense that she becomes intense at all.

IF A WOMAN cares for a man she will never give him away; she will not even lend him to a friend.

IT IS not enough for a woman to wear her clothes well, she must also wear well herself.

IT IS hardly fair to say that women are inherently deceitful. No woman ever concealed anything that she dared reveal.

SOME women are capable of doing anything for the man they love, others make the man they love capable of doing anything.

THE only criterion for choosing presents is one's own taste; that is why old ladies give their nephews pin cushions, children give their parents toys, men give their wives cigars, and lovers give each other kisses.

IT IS not the woman the man she loves has kissed that should worry a jealous woman but the women he has not kissed—yet.

YOU would be astonished at the calculations the most unmathematical woman can do in her head.

THE man who may mayn't, the man who mayn't will every time.

ONE'S friends are divided into two classes, those one knows because one must and those one knows because one mustn't.

MANY a woman who seems to want coaxing might be driven if the car were luxurious enough.

IN THE game of life the woman who is lucky in hearts generally holds the biggest diamonds too.

TO BE subject to one's relations is worse than being subject to fits.

ONLY the novice attempts to fascinate a man by convincing him how charming she is; the woman who knows simply convinces him how charming he is and the rest just happens.

THERE are some men whose very insolence is flattery to a woman, while even the flattery of others is insulting.

SOME women seem to think that they have only to wear a smile to be chic.

WOMAN has proved that she can take a man's place among men. But she will never be able to take a man's place among women.

LOVE is like a bazaar. The admittance is free but it costs you something before you get out.

NARROW minds seem to be able to squeeze in anywhere.

IT IS difficult enough to know the right people, but a hundred times more difficult to love the right people.

EVERYONE has been young once, most women are young about three times.

IT IS hard to say which is the more to be pitied, a man with an ugly, unattractive wife he does not care for or the man with a pretty fascinating wife whom he does care for.

NO ONE has anything but contempt for the world's opinion of them—unless it is a really good one.

A WOMAN has to choose between being an episode and being a nuisance.

SPEECH may have been given a woman to conceal her thoughts but clothes were certainly not given her to conceal her form.

THE fact that he is boring other people luckily does not prevent a man from amusing himself.

PEOPLE who have lost their reputation generally acquire such very bad ones in its place.

AS LONG as you return his presents a man will continue to love you, but return his love and he really does become discouraged.

MANY a woman tries to cheer herself up with the thought that her husband would be sorry if she died.

THE husband who counts is the one who has something to count.

A GIRL must sometimes find it awfully difficult to give her friends a good reason for having married the only man who ever asked her.

GOOD women are nearly always jealous of bad women—and they have every reason to be.

IF A MAN loves his wife he thinks everyone does, and if he does not love her he thinks no one does—and in both cases he is probably wrong.

THREE is usually an unlucky number if one is the third.

HOME comforts are things that are always sent to people away from home; those at home have to put up with the discomforts.

A MAN is really capable if he can successfully mix his wines and keep his women friends apart.

A MAN does not love a woman because she is a good house-keeper, but he is quite likely to unlove her because she is a bad one.

TO HAVE their private life made public is the way some people have got into and others out of society.

FROM the way some people seem to avoid knowing themselves we imagine them to be quite particular about their acquaintances.

YOU may feel for others but you must think for yourself.

ALMOST anyone can see the humour of the situation when it is someone else who is situated.

THE very worst people often live at the very best addresses.

A MAN of honour does not help himself to another man's property—until he can't help himself.

SO MANY people would give anything to escape from home to some place where they could be really at home.

LOVE has so many components—multi-coloured beads threaded on the string of trust; break that and all the beads are scattered.

THAT a man is fat does not necessarily prove that he is generous—except to himself.

THERE are people who are always complaining that they don't know what to do, while the only trouble other people have is that they can't remember what not to do.

EVERY woman acts one part in her life, that of the sort of girl the man she wants to marry wants to marry.

WOMEN are divided into two classes, good wives who have no husband, and bad wives who have several.

GOODNESS only knows—half what wickedness knows.

THERE are all sorts of women. Choose one you like, but never try to change the one you choose.

A PRETTY girl can afford to wear inexpensive dresses, on the other hand she is more likely to be able to afford costly ones than if she were plain.

AN INNOCENT question may have anything but an innocent answer.

WHEN a flapper wants to she does, when she doesn't want to she says her mother wo'nt let her.

IT IS USELESS to be able to support a woman in luxury if you cannot support her *en déshabille*.

WOMEN love men for what they give them, men love women for what they deny them.

BETTER a will in your favour than a will of your own.

THE ONLY way to keep a man at home is to go out with him.

A MAN is like an omelette, he cannot be successfully warmed up again once he has got cold.

NEVER make a woman cry unless she insists.

'TRUE FRIENDS' are generally quite impossible, and true lovers highly improbable.

THE TROUBLE is that man is by nature a man—not a husband.

WHEN you see an old man alone you are looking at something very sad. When you see an old man with a young woman you are looking at something rich.

TO KNOW and understand women requires brain: to know and understand men requires beauty.

YOU NEED not consider a man but you must amuse him.

WHEN a woman begins to boast of the insults she has been offered in the past her charms are waning.

THERE are no middle-aged people now: they are young, wonderful for their age, and then dead.

A CLEVER woman can help her husband, a pretty woman can help herself.

A WOMAN never notices that there is nothing to do in a place unless there is no one to do it with.

MOONLIGHT does not make things happen but it makes them visible.

THERE IS a lot of difference between the man who admires fresh complexions and the man who likes fresh faces.

THE history of the world is the story of how different people made the same mistake. Progress is the occasional departure from this order when someone has sufficient genius to think of a new sort of mistake to make.

MEN never grow up, they begin and end in arms.

THE ACT of 'putting your cards on the table' does not necessarily reveal what your foot is doing under it.

IF A WOMAN wants a thing she gets it. If a man wants a thing he buys it.

OPINIONS differ as to whether it is bad to be modern or merely modern to be bad.

WOMEN will destroy a man's faith, his illusions, his love: but they will *not* destroy his letters.

A MAN goes to a woman when he is in trouble—and gets into more trouble.

VERY few women will go so far to prove that their price is above rubies as to refuse —rubies.

SOME people who boast of not wearing their heart on their sleeve probably know that if they did it would give them a most awfully shabby appearance.

WHEN a man has money to burn the chronic borrower is a match for him.

THERE are people who read books, look at cathedrals and commit sins merely to provide themselves with topics of conversation.

MOST women look better on a cushioned couch than on a pedestal, and certainly feel more at home.

FIRE-ARMS and freedom are two things that very few women ever handle properly.

WHEN a woman wants a man to love her it does not necessarily mean that she loves him; it probably means that some other woman loves him.

NO WOMAN with real beauty ever had false modesty.

WHAT a woman doesn't know she guesses, and what she guesses she knows.

PEOPLE will tell you that they never do what they are ashamed of, when what they really mean is that they are never ashamed of what they do.

WOMAN is the eternal question, and man is the answer to it.

A WOMAN should exercise the greatest care in the choice of the men she allows to love her, for by the quality of her lovers the quality of her attractions will be judged.

ORIGINALLY an animal, man has been improved by civilization and may eventually develop into a perfect beast.

A MAN who will come and go at a woman's word invariably has to go once oftener than he comes.

IF A WOMAN speaks without thinking, she may perhaps say what she really thinks.

A MAN'S sense of honour is a very delicate mechanism and apt to get out of order if brought too near a pretty woman.

TO LOOK WELL DRESSED is a matter of technique; to look well undressed requires natural gifts.

WHAT a woman wears reveals more than
what she says.

A WOMAN'S KISSES prove almost as little as her words. A man kisses a woman because she attracts him, while a woman kisses a man because she likes to attract him.

FEW MEN are quite so intolerable as the eulogies of the women who love them make them out to be.

A LOVER'S eyes are a flattering mirror.

IT IS NOT quite fair to blame people for not possessing the virtues with which your imagination has endowed them.

CONVERSATION IS listening to yourself in the presence of others.

THE TRUE test is not whether a man behaves like a gentleman, but whether he misbehaves like one.

A WOMAN loses her illusions at just about the same time as she loses her looks.

A MAN'S IDEA of 'life' is a series of improbable situations with impossible people.

SO MANY rich men have given up all the pleasures of youth so that when they are old they can afford all the things they can no longer enjoy.

MOST MARRIED people would get on so much better together if they were apart.

A MAN will tell a woman that he loves her for herself alone, but what he really means is that he loves her for himself alone.

A WOMAN'S chief asset lies in what is invested with mystery; a man's chief assets must needs be invested with knowledge.

NOW-A-DAYS it is almost impossible to keep outsiders outside.

MOST PEOPLE'S idea of 'starting afresh' is going on in the same way somewhere else.

IT IS the man with plenty of cash who gets plenty of change.

WHEN A woman marries she displays her ability to do so. When a man marries he displays his inability not to do so.

IN MARRIAGE or any other adversity a nice man's best points come out, which is very delightful as long as his teeth are not his best point.

NO MAN ever regrets resisting temptation, because no man ever resists a temptation.

A MAN kisses whom he may and loves whom he mayn't.

NEVER ask a man—just make him tell you.

RED haired women generally look as if they would like to be kissed, while red haired men look as if they would like to be bald.

YOU CANNOT make a young girl's interest grow by pouring lotion on a bald head.

THE book of life is illustrated in black and white; dreams are the colour supplement.

THE most tragic moment of a woman's life is the one in which she realises that she can at last play with fire without getting burnt.

WHEN a woman believes in a man's fidelity it is not because she trusts him, but because she has confidence in herself.

MOST women start a love affair by having a secret with a man, and end by having secrets from him.

THERE are not enough men to go round, but some heroes attempt to put things right by going round as much as ever they can.

MOST people would like their own ways and other people's means.

SUCCESSFUL men take advantage of opportunities—successful women take advantage of successful men.

THE object of a woman with a past is probably a man with a present.

IT IS a woman's lot to pretend to care less than she does, while a man pretends to care more than he does. They both leave off pretending about the same time.

MEN have privileges—but they have to pay the cab.